YOU ARE A COSMIC TREE

Dear Williams Family,

We visited the Bahai temple in Chicago — so beautiful! And loved their message of inclusivity ♡

Love you guys!

X. The Boiedu Family

YOU ARE A COSMIC TREE

MISHA MAYNERICK BLAISE

BELLWOOD PRESS®

EVANSTON, ILLINOIS

Bellwood Press, Evanston, Illinois
1233 Central Street, Evanston, Illinois 60201
Copyright © 2024 by the National Spiritual Assembly
of the Baháʼís of the United States
All rights reserved. Published 2024.
Printed in the United States of America
on acid-free paper ∞

27 26 25 24   4 3 2 1

Library of Congress Cataloging-in-Publication Data

Names: Blaise, Misha Maynerick, 1977- author.
Title: You are a cosmic tree : Baháʼí-inspired art & reflections on the life of the soul / Misha Maynerick Blaise.
Description: Evanston, Illinois : Bellwood Press, 2024. | Includes bibliographical references. | Summary: "You Are a Cosmic Tree blends art, humor, and the deep wisdom of the Baháʼí teachings in a captivating visual journey into the life of the soul. Exploring concepts such as prayer and meditation, tests and difficulties, and our relationship with God, readers are invited to see life as a process of spiritual transformation and growth. The cosmic tree is a mythical symbol that represents the connection between the physical and the spiritual, the body and soul. Your true self is an eternal soul embodied in a human experience, one that is connected to others through our one human family. Amidst the turmoil of our times, You Are a Cosmic Tree offers teens and adults a joyful artistic odyssey into a hopeful worldview grounded in the sacred teachings of a dynamic global religion"-- Provided by publisher.
Identifiers: LCCN 2024038983 (print) | LCCN 2024038984 (ebook) | ISBN 9781618512574 (paperback) | ISBN 9781618512581 (ebook)
Subjects: LCSH: Bahai Faith--Spiritual life. | Prayer--Bahai Faith.
Classification: LCC BP380 .B53 2024 (print) | LCC BP380 (ebook) | DDC 297.9/3--dc23/eng/20240904
LC record available at https://lccn.loc.gov/2024038983
LC ebook record available at https://lccn.loc.gov/2024038984

CONTENTS

Important Note vi
Introduction 2
1 / The Life of the Soul 12
2 / The Soul's Relationship with God 38
3 / Tests and Difficulties 52
4 / How to Transform 72
5 / The Journey of Humanity 94
6 / The Two-Fold Moral Purpose 118
Conclusion 132
Where Do These Bahá'í Writings Come From? 139
Thank You 141
Afterword 143
Notes 147
Bibliography 153

IMPORTANT NOTE

The cosmic tree is a universal symbol found in cultural mythologies worldwide. It represents the connection between the physical and spiritual realms and embodies the vast mysteries of existence. The cosmic tree portrays life's interconnectedness, from the smallest particles to the largest galaxies.

You ARE A COSMIC TREE.

"Make me a brilliant lamp,
a shining star and a blessed tree,
adorned with fruit, its branches
overshadowing all these regions."

—'Abdu'l-Bahá[1]

INTRODUCTION

HEY tHERE!

You are a person living on Earth right now. You get to be here for a while with several BILLION other people!

The era we are living in is a unique and powerful time in human history for one simple reason:

IT IS NOW POSSIBLE TO RECOGNIZE THE ONENESS of HUMANITY!

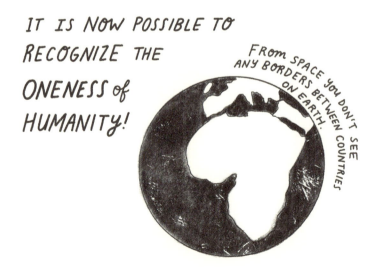

From SPACE you don't see any BORDERS BETWEEN COUNTRIES ON EARTH.

Suddenly, in a relatively small scope of time, the world's people have been flung together into a global society.

SO MANY THINGS CONNECT US AS A GLOBAL COMMUNITY!

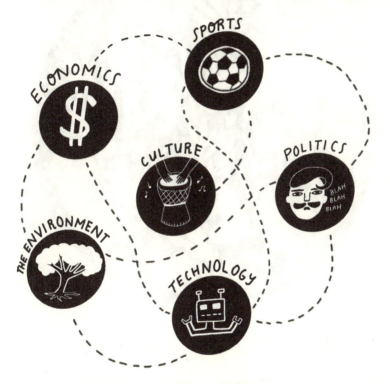

ETC., ETC., ETC.

People from totally different cultures are intertwined in each other's lives and influence each other in millions of different ways.

This is a time of great transition, filled with both turmoil and possibility. From one perspective, it seems like the world is worse now than it has ever been. From another view, in many ways the world is doing better than it ever has in history.

Amidst the competing ideologies and social divisions of our era, there is one fact that stands out: We are one human family sharing a single planetary homeland.

THERE IS NO "US" AND "THEM": THERE IS ONLY US.

More and more people are recognizing the essential oneness of humanity and long for a world that is more safe, just, and peaceful.

We each live in this world, with our own fears, hopes, and beliefs. Worldviews create worlds; our inner cosmology impacts our outer life. The way you make sense of things impacts your experience in the world and how you choose to live your life.

This book is about exploring big ideas from the Bahá'í writings about the life of the soul, what it means to be human, and how to find your true self in an age of rapid change.

Amidst the uncertainty of our times, we need a clear way to make sense of what is happening in our own life and in the world around us. The Bahá'í teachings offer a whole new way of looking at things that helps inspire faith in the goodness of life, and the courage to bring our own goodness into the world.

The universe is immense and complex, which suggests an immense complexity to your own soul. Like a cosmic tree whose roots and branches grow in every direction for all eternity, your life is one of unending growth and development.

And because we are all interconnected, your own journey of self-discovery is connected with the ever-unfolding story of humanity. This book is an invitation to look through a spiritual lens and see life as a big sacred thing that you are always part of.

The Bahá'í Faith encourages every person to seek truth for themselves. You can use your own mind and heart to investigate reality. It's your birthright to ask all the questions you want and search for answers that make sense to you!

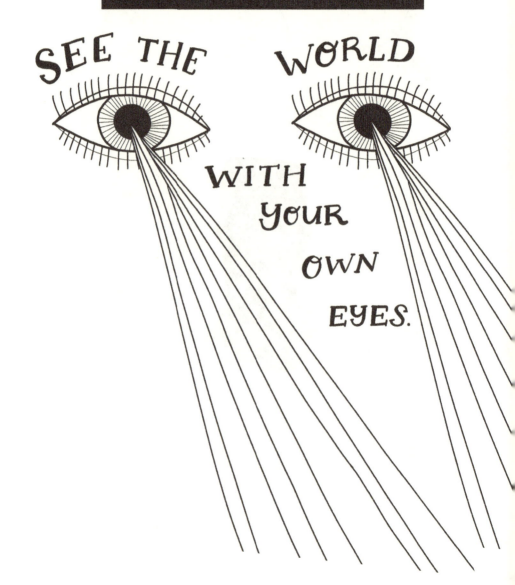

THIS IS YOUR ONE LIFE. NO ONE CAN LIVE IT FOR YOU!

Each person is responsible to bravely step out on their own spiritual journey.

The world is filled with deep mysteries that unfold across a lifetime. As you chart your course through an ever-changing world, the Bahá'í teachings are a reminder that you belong here, and there is hope even in the hardship.

CHAPTER ONE

THE LIFE OF THE SOUL

Every single atom in our bodies was once part of a star, and when those stars went supernova, they spread their cosmic magic, creating the elements that eventually formed the Earth and everything on it.[3]

The entire physical universe is bound together in a state of oneness. A tree could not exist without rain, rain could not form without clouds, clouds could not form without the atmosphere, and you could not exist without any of these things. When we view the world with this concept of interconnection in our minds, we remember that all of creation is a part of us, and we are at one with all things.

"... all the members of this endless universe are linked one to another."

—'Abdu'l-Bahá[4]

WE SHARE AN ANCIENT COSMIC HERITAGE WITH **EVERYTHING!**

The whole universe conspired to create you!
Your existence is part of the movement of the cosmos.
You weren't born in the wrong time or place.

You were created in the burning heart of the universe, and

YOU WERE <u>MADE</u> FOR THIS <u>MOMENT</u>!

It's an incredible miracle that you are alive right now! Since modern humans emerged about 200,000 years ago, about 7,000 generations have come and gone, leading up to your ONE LIFE.

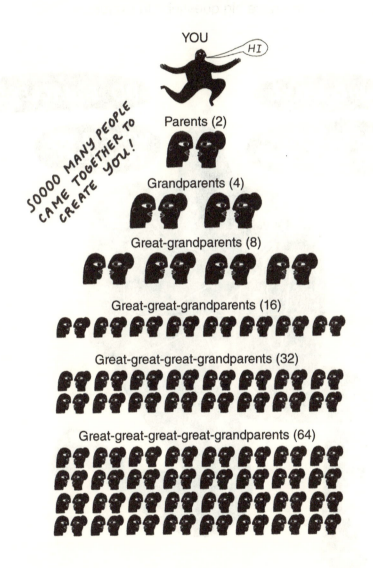

Tens of thousands of people lived out their own epic dramas that led to your emergence. Within just five generations, sixty-four people's lives had to align perfectly to eventually result in your birth!

Now that you are here,
you have big questions to explore.

We each have an inner world that influences our experience of life and how we make sense of things. The Bahá'í Faith calls this innermost self the soul. It represents the most authentic aspect of our being; it's who we are at the most profound level.

We don't know exactly what the soul is. The Bahá'í teachings say it is *"entirely out of the order of the physical creation."*[5] But we can use metaphor as a bridge between the mystery of the soul and our tangible human experience.

Our soul is like the trunk and roots of a tree. A trunk serves as the central core and support of the tree, just as the soul is the spiritual foundation upon which our identity is built. The roots give nourishment and stability to the tree, reflecting the wellspring of deeper wisdom that your soul can always tap into.

Each branch splits into smaller branches, which later split into twigs. The branches represent different facets of our identity. Some are innate; others are shaped by our experiences, relationships, and cultural influences; and many are a combination of both nature and nurture.

While these branches may represent important aspects of our worldly identity, it is essential to recognize that they are dependent upon the structure of the sturdy trunk: the deeper wisdom and essence of the soul.

Sometimes people get confused and think that their true identity is just one of the little twigs.

People can invest a lifetime into their twig-self, and therefore miss the opportunity to explore the trunk of their soul, where a deeper experience of life is found.

The soul is a divine spark, a fundamental and eternal reality. It's your most essential identity, beneath the surface layers of your personality, social connections, or family role. It encompasses all of who you are and who you could be.

The soul is like an inner universe, an expansive wilderness that's vast beyond belief. It's an almost entirely unknown territory, but you are free to explore it as deeply as you can. There are treasures hidden there, waiting to be unearthed. You wander through its sunlight and shadows, its heights and depths, but its full reality is beyond comprehension.

The Bahá'í Faith teaches that the soul is on an eternal journey of growth and transformation.

Human life is a combination of body and soul. In this earthly life, you are a mix of divine qualities and earthly experiences. You have both physical and spiritual powers.

Your physical senses take in information about the world around you.

HEARING
SIGHT
SMELL
TASTE
TOUCH

VIBES

The soul can be thought of as a set of powers that allow you to make meaning of your physical perceptions.

THE POWERS OF THE SOUL

(a few examples)

The power of the mind:
the ability to gain knowledge and seek understanding.

The power of the will:
the ability to have agency and take action.

The power of the heart:
the ability to feel emotion, connection, and love.

The power of imagination:
the ability to create new ideas.

The powers of the soul release all the arts, sciences, and innovations of humanity. From the absolute darkness of realms unknown, these powers bring forth what was previously unseen into the world of light.

Humans cannot fly. Yet the powers of the mind made flight possible!

Humans cannot breathe under water. Yet we can survive in the depths of the ocean!

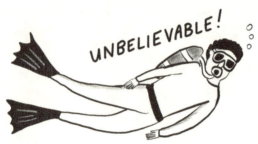

Humans need food to survive. We invented a rice cooker to make perfect rice!

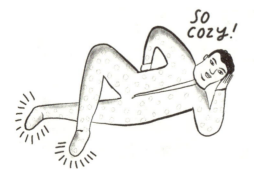

Humans need warmth. Behold: We innovated footie pajamas!

The soul holds endless potential for creativity, conjuring things we never could have expected.

THE SOUL ACtS IN tHE PHYSICAL WORLD WItH tHE HELP of the BODY.

—attributed to 'Abdu'l-Bahá[6]

When we tap into the powers of the soul, we can experience spiritual growth. Spiritual growth is a dynamic and lifelong process that involves developing spiritual qualities such as love, generosity, patience, self-sacrifice, sincerity, discernment, justice, empathy, humility, courage, and kindness. These virtues bring out the best version of yourself and help create a more just and loving world.

The nature of our material world is one of constant change and impermanence. At a cellular level, we are always changing. Our seemingly solid bodies are vibrating with the movement of trillions of cells, all of which have a limited life span.

AVERAGE LIFE SPANS OF ASSORTED CELLS:

CELLS THAT LINE THE INTESTINE

three to five days

RED BLOOD CELLS

about four months

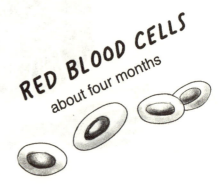

CELLS IN YOUR SKELETAL SYSTEM

about ten years

UPPER LAYER SKIN CELLS

two to four weeks

As old cells die off, your body creates new cells to take their place. Your body is literally dying and being reborn every moment.

Material life is characterized by impermanence and change. But the Bahá'í teachings assure us that even though our bodies wither and decline, the soul can only progress.

The Bahá'í writings describe the soul and body as having a relationship similar to that of light reflected in a mirror. A bright light can be perfectly reflected in a clear mirror. But if the mirror breaks, it does not harm the source of the light. Similarly, the light of the soul transcends the limitations of the body. The essence of the soul is everlasting![7]

Your unique, individuated soul associates with your body at the time of conception but it is not part of your body. It is not material; it has no physical qualities. When you die, your body disintegrates, but your soul is on an eternal journey.

Another metaphor for the soul is that of a baby in the womb. Similar to how a baby develops in the womb in preparation for this life, your soul develops in the "womb" of this physical universe in preparation for its birth into the next world, a more expansive spiritual reality.

When a fetus is in the womb, she is living in a totally different realm from this one. And all her development in that limited condition is part of a trajectory toward another realm of existence.

THIS STUFF IS NOT USEFUL IN THE WOMB:

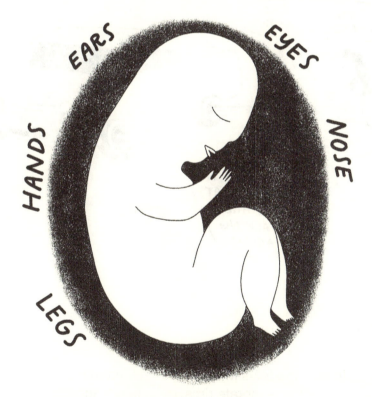

ETC., ETC., ETC...

All these body parts are developed in the womb, but they don't find their full expression until the baby enters this world.

If you could somehow tell the fetus something about this world—that there are delicious enchiladas, beautiful sunsets, and that some people put elaborate rims on their cars—none of this would make any sense; she would have absolutely no point of reference.

In fact, the fetus may never understand the point of the elaborate rims, even in adulthood!

The world of the womb is a different dimension, but simultaneously it's enveloped by this world, separated from us by only a thin layer of skin.

ACTUALLY, I DON'T BELIEVE IN LIFE AFTER DELIVERY.

Similar to how the baby in the womb is already enveloped by this world, our soul is somehow already enveloped by the next world, but that realm is so different that we have no way to comprehend it.

Death, therefore, is a transition from one stage of existence to another along a continual spiritual evolution.

The soul is a dynamic, ever-evolving entity. Life here on Earth is just one stage of an endless journey. And whatever we are going though, there is always somewhere to turn for comfort, relief, and guidance.

CHAPTER TWO

THE SOUL'S RELATIONSHIP WITH GOD

Have you ever thought about how crazy it is to be alive within the greater scheme of things? Right now, we humans are all floating together on a tiny planet that is part of a larger solar system that rotates around the center of the Milky Way Galaxy, which is just one of at least 100 billion galaxies that make up the observable universe. We are basically on a piece of dust floating through infinity.

QUIZ
(CHECK ONE)

How does it feel right now to be an infinitesimally small creature floating on a speck of dust through an infinitude?

- ☐ *INCREDIBLE!*
- ☐ *TERRIFYING!*
- ☐ *HADN'T NOTICED.*

Have you ever looked into the night sky and thought about life's big questions?

The word **"YUGEN"** in Japanese means:

"AN AWARENESS OF THE UNIVERSE THAT TRIGGERS FEELINGS TOO DEEP AND MYSTERIOUS FOR WORDS."

Basically, the fact of our existence is a mystery wrapped in a mystery. Which is then wrapped in an even bigger, juicier, more deep-fried mystery!

Humans are wired to make sense of things. It's one of our soul's great powers! It's normal to be curious about your relationship with every other thing,

both the knowable: 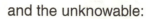 and the unknowable:

We are compelled to explore the mysteries of existence.

The Ultimate Mystery of the universe is called by many names: Alláh, the Great Spirit, God, or the Primal Source. The Bahá'í Faith affirms that the reality of God is totally incomprehensible, an "Unknowable Essence" that humans can never fathom.[8]

We are limited in our physical capacities; our eyes can't see beyond a certain point on the light spectrum; our ears can't hear beyond certain frequencies. It makes sense that our minds can't fathom the ultimate source of all existence.

And yet at the same time, the Bahá'í Faith describes God's intimate closeness:

"This most great, this fathomless and surging Ocean is near, astonishingly near, unto you. Behold it is closer to you than your life-vein!"

— Bahá'u'lláh[9]

God is here, right now, and He knows us, cares about us, and is more intimately intertwined with our existence than our own life-vein. The journey of the soul is seen as an eternal progression toward closeness with God.

Here is a small glimpse into the many different titles and attributes of God found in the Bahá'í writings:

The paradox of God's unknowable mystery and immediate closeness is a catalyst for spiritual exploration and growth. How can something so vast and unimaginable be so intimate and personal?

The Bahá'í writings say that the heart of religious faith is the mystical feeling that connects the individual with God.[10] "Mystical feeling" doesn't mean something paranormal or ghosty. It refers to a profound sense of connection to God through the power of transcendent love.

Love is more than an idea. We feel it in our bodies and in our hearts. Bahá'u'lláh calls the heart: "The seat of the revelation of the inner mysteries of God."[11]

For example, *takotsubo cardiomyopathy* is a medical condition where the heart loses strength and temporarily changes shape in reaction to an emotional trigger (This condition is named after the *takotsubo*, a Japanese pot with a wide base and narrow neck).[12]

Interestingly, the heart can change shape in reaction to severe grief, anger, or stress, but it can also change in times of great joy. Takotsubo cardiomyopathy has therefore been given the nickname "broken heart syndrome" as well as "happy heart syndrome." The physical heart informs us of our true feelings; through it we powerfully experience both pain and love.

'Abdu'l-Bahá calls love "the secret of God's holy Dispensation." Love is the primal force that creates and sustains all of creation. We are brought forth out of nothingness through the power of love. All existence is a reflection of divine love.

Through this lens of love we can reconceptualize the organization of the whole universe. Love is the strong force that joins subatomic particles together, love is the gravity that holds the planets in orbit around the sun.

"Love is the cause of God's revelation unto man . . . the most great law that ruleth this mighty and heavenly cycle, the unique power that bindeth together the diverse elements of this material world."

—'Abdu'l-Bahá[13]

Maybe you connect with that love through nature, a meaningful relationship, or the process of creating art. The mystical longing of the soul is that deep desire you have to experience what is most real and true about life.

Material comforts, money, and status can contribute to a comfortable and secure life, but to feel real contentment, the inner world needs to be valued. The Bahá'í writings say that progress is of two kinds, material and spiritual, and we should seek coherence between the two.[14] The soul desires self-discovery, meaningful connections, true belonging, beauty, and authenticity. The soul wants to feel the rapture and delight of being alive!

With the mystic love of God at the center
of the soul's journey, you are guided in unexpected ways
toward a deeper connection with life itself. This sacred
relationship with God feeds the soul and unleashes the
virtues and powers that are stored up within you.
It can help you see other people
and the world itself in a new light.

Recognizing that your life is embraced
by the mystical love of God can
reshape how you relate to the
challenges and suffering inherent in
the human experience.

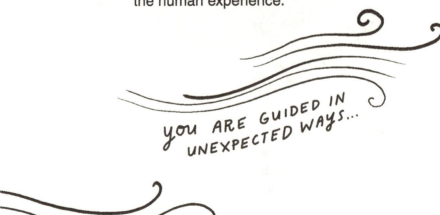

you ARE GUIDED IN UNEXPECTED WAYS...

CHAPTER THREE

TESTS AND DIFFICULTIES

TESTS AND DIFFICULTIES

Life is like a training ground where your soul can learn about love. Life is designed to stimulate the powers of your soul as you experience all the challenges, joys, paradoxes, and mysteries the world has to offer.

We can look at the miracle of existence
with a feeling of deep wonder and gratitude.

For example: Romanesco broccoli is shaped like a fractal!

Likewise, every hardship can be seen
as an opportunity to learn and grow.

But this attitude is not easy, especially when things are hard. Even though the soul is a wondrous expanse of unlimited potential, it doesn't always feel that way. When situations in life get extremely difficult, when you feel stressed beyond your capacity to handle things, your soul gets tested.

Bahá'u'lláh teaches that the soul has the power to persevere and struggle through pain, and that the soul will never be tested beyond its ability to withstand.

"Thou wert created to bear and endure, O Patience of the worlds"

—Bahá'u'lláh[15]

You are destined to face all the ups and downs of the human condition. Mortality, sickness, loss, suffering, and death are all your close companions. You will feel things in life: good things, bad things, confusing things, scary things, fluffy things.

YOU WILL FEEL ALL the THINGS!

To develop spiritually, you do not need to deny difficult emotions or ignore feelings of fear, anxiety, grief, or anger. Often, it is through honestly facing these unsettling feelings that we learn about ourselves and determine to set out on a path of true healing and growth. Painful emotions can give you important information about your needs, fears, and beliefs.

Probably the worst thing you can tell someone who is facing difficulty is that it is all part of some larger process of positive growth. That kind of talk comes off as super annoying and dismissive:

THERE IS A MAGICAL UNICORN OF **HOPE** LEAPING ACROSS THE DECOMPOSING TRASH PILE OF YOUR TRAGEDY!

And yet, suffering is woven into the fabric of human experience. It is a profound truth that can potentially bring wisdom and insight into the nature of existence.

**"It is only through suffering that
the nobility of character
can make itself manifest."**

—Shoghi Effendi[16]

If there were no unknowns in life, there would be no doubt or anxiety. With no doubt or anxiety, there would be no need for faith, courage, and effort. Great and terrible challenges can cause you to draw upon the latent powers of resilience and healing deep within your soul. A famous Zen proverb says:

"THE OBSTACLE IS THE PATH."[17]

Suffering is therefore not a punishment or an act of God's wrath; rather, it is a primal force that can unleash your creative powers and help you turn toward God. It may not always be possible to make sense of things, but we can try to courageously engage the chaos, darkness, and hurt that are part of the human condition.

And we are never left alone in our suffering:

> **"Turn thy sight unto thyself, that thou mayest find Me standing within thee, mighty, powerful and self-subsisting."**
>
> — Bahá'u'lláh[18]

Suffering is something that all people experience at some point. At the same time, it's also our moral duty to try and alleviate unnecessary suffering in the world so that people don't have to face unjust burdens and hardship. Often our own experiences with a certain issue can inform how we want to give back to the world. We might be inspired to help others who face the same difficulty, or we can take broader social action to transform the source of a problem.

The inner struggle between your own lower and higher nature is often what sparks the soul's opportunity for growth.

THE DYNAMIC TENSION BETWEEN YOUR LOWER AND HIGHER NATURE

Within each of us is a dynamic tension between our higher nature and a lower nature.

The higher nature is home to your spiritual qualities. These include things like love, generosity, patience, self-sacrifice, sincerity, discernment, justice, connection, empathy, humility, courage, and kindness.

The lower nature can dominate your personality when you neglect these spiritual qualities. This results in things like selfishness, greed, lying, hatred, jealousy, ignorance, meanness, prejudice, or cruelty.

The lower nature reflects the human tendency to indulge selfish desires and live for material gratification alone. Our lower nature can trap us in limited, cynical, or pessimistic ways of looking at the world. It can close our hearts off to love and cause us to fall into nihilism or despair. In trying to avoid pain, fear, or uncertainty, our lower nature seeks comfort in shallow distractions, addiction, and escape. Our lower nature can cause us to lash out and bring pain to ourselves and others as we continue cycles of violence.

> "In man there are two natures; his spiritual or higher nature and his material or lower nature. In one he approaches God, in the other he lives for the world alone. Signs of both these natures are to be found in men."
>
> — 'Abdu'l-Bahá[19]

This inner conflict between our high ideals and our limiting shortcomings is no accident. By cosmic design, our higher nature and our lower nature are in perpetual tension with one another.

Just as a bird uses the strength of its wings to resist gravity and soar into the air, we must work to develop our higher spiritual virtues against the forces of our lower nature that pull us down.

It is in this context that the Bahá'í writings define heaven and hell—not as physical places, but as conditions of the soul in relationship to God. To feel cut off from God and trapped in your lower nature is hell, to feel close to God and connected to your higher nature is heaven.

**"Where is Paradise, and where is Hell? . . .
The one is reunion with Me;
the other thine own self."**

—Bahá'u'lláh[20]

"Ultimately all the battle of life is within the individual."

—Shoghi Effendi[21]

Every person on earth confronts this fundamental struggle between the higher and lower nature. The goal is not to transcend being human or escape the stuff of life, for we are imperfect and can never know or understand everything. The point is rather to be honest with yourself about your own struggles and strive to develop your higher nature as a force of wisdom and compassion.

This includes compassion with oneself.
Many people struggle with the voice of the inner critic—
the little perfectionist tyrant that hovers over your life
and incessantly shames, judges, and berates you.

This mean inner tyrant needs to be replaced by a kind inner friend. The inner friend is curious about your experience and can be self-compassionate even in the face of your mistakes and shortcomings. This attitude promotes learning and growth. It also makes it easier to empathize with others if you have empathy for yourself.

> " ... man should know his own self and recognize that which leadeth unto loftiness or lowliness, glory or abasement, wealth or poverty."

—Baháʼu'lláh[22]

It would be easier to express our higher nature if we were all perfect angelic robots with no power of choice. However, we are human, and each of us has the gift of free will. Each one of us can choose how we want to direct our own energy and attention.

Although we have personal responsibility, the way we are educated by our family and greater society can also serve to bring out our lower or higher nature. We are like plants and our family and culture are the ecosystem we grow up in. We need the right soil, light, and water to help bring out our best self.

Our lower nature is like the ground against which the flower of our higher nature can push and grow. By struggling in opposition to our lower nature, our higher nature gains wisdom and insight. Paradoxically, the tension between the higher and lower nature is the impetus for spiritual development.

"OUR CAPACITY to DESTROY ONE ANOTHER IS MATCHED BY OUR CAPACITY to HEAL ONE ANOTHER."

—Bessel van der Kolk, trauma specialist[23]

Through self-reflection and grappling with the shadows that linger in the crevices of your consciousness, you can increase spiritual perception and resilience. Day by day, facing the tension within can lead to greater self-awareness.

CHAPTER FOUR

HOW TO TRANSFORM

The Word of God is often referred to as

THE CREATIVE WORD

because of its power to change and renew us.[24]

As we explore the Bahá'í writings, we start to understand ourselves in a new way. We build a new framework for how to make sense of the world. Our way of thinking shapes how we feel and behave. This impacts our relationships, which in turn influences the culture around us.
The very purpose of religion is spiritual transformation.

> "... The Word is the master key for the whole world, inasmuch as through its potency the doors of the hearts of men, which in reality are the doors of heaven, are unlocked..."
>
> —Bahá'u'lláh[25]

Immersion in the ocean of Bahá'u'lláh's words can give you a "new life," and it can totally reframe the way you look at being human and the times you are living in.[26]

It's impossible to know ahead of time how the Word of God will impact you. The soul is always in a process of development, and there are no limits on how much you can grow, learn, love, and contribute to the world.

Prayer and meditation are tools that can open your soul to the power of the creative word.

PRAYER AND MEDITATION ARE YOUR SUPERPOWERS

God created every wonder of the universe, including you! The cosmos is vast and inexplicable, so it makes sense that there are unknown and untapped possibilities within your own soul.

"I CONTAIN MULTITUDES." —WALT WHITMAN [27]

Prayer and meditation are tools that illuminate your inner world and release your soul's potential. Similar to how you need good food and exercise to help you stay physically healthy, prayer and meditation support your spiritual development.

If this world is a spiritual world of God, it means that you can live in a state of prayer no matter where you are or what you are doing! For example, you can live in a state of prayer . . .

At the gym

While eating a piece of pizza with a hotdog-stuffed crust

While folding laundry

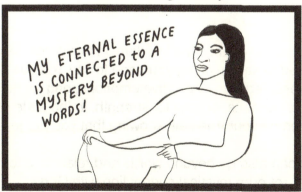

Prayer can be thought of as your own personal conversation with God. In this sense, it supports the relationship between you and your Creator. And this relationship is fundamentally based on love.

"I loved thy creation, hence I created thee. Wherefore, do thou love Me, that I may name thy name and fill thy soul with the spirit of life."

— Bahá'u'lláh[28]

Prayer is a space of absolute freedom: in this conversation you are allowed to say anything you need to say. You can ask for help, express negative or positive emotions, beg for guidance, release your burdens, or pray for strength. In the state of prayer you can be your true self, knowing that you are loved.

Prayer can also go beyond words and relate to a feeling of pure mystical connection with God.

'Abdu'l-Bahá describes this as "a prayer that shall rise above words and letters and transcend the murmur of syllables and sounds—that all things may be merged into nothingness before the revelation of Thy [God's] splendor."[29]

Through communion with God, the Bahá'í writings speak of a "mystic transformation"[30] that brings inner peace, certitude, and courage.

Even if situations are difficult, prayer can bring a shift in perspective that can refresh the spirit and illuminate new paths on which to move forward.

"There is nothing sweeter in the world of existence than prayer. Man must live in a state of prayer. The most blessed condition is the condition of prayer and supplication."

—attributed to 'Abdu'l-Bahá[31]

But prayer is much more than silent contemplation. 'Abdu'l-Bahá says, "Strive that your actions day by day may be beautiful prayers."³² The way we live our lives can be a prayer. Working hard, serving others, helping a friend, or creating a piece of art can all be considered prayers if done in a spirit of love and devotion.

Likewise, meditation is an intentional shift in awareness that allows you to connect with your inner self. Although the Bahá'í writings don't prescribe any specific technique, 'Abdu'l-Bahá describes meditation as a means for accessing deep insight:

"Meditation is the key for opening the doors of mysteries. In that state man abstracts himself: in that state man withdraws himself from all outside objects; in that subjective mood he is immersed in the ocean of spiritual life and can unfold the secrets of things-in-themselves..."[33]

The practice of prayer and meditation can orient your thoughts toward high ideals, open your heart to love, and strengthen your reliance on God. This, in turn, can affect your perception of the world. Modern neuroscience shows that your habits of thought have a profound impact on the way you experience and interact with the world.

PRAYER AND NEUROPLASTICITY

One of the most exciting breakthroughs in brain science in the past century is the discovery that the brain has an innate power to change, adapt, and restructure itself in response to its environment. This is known as neuroplasticity.

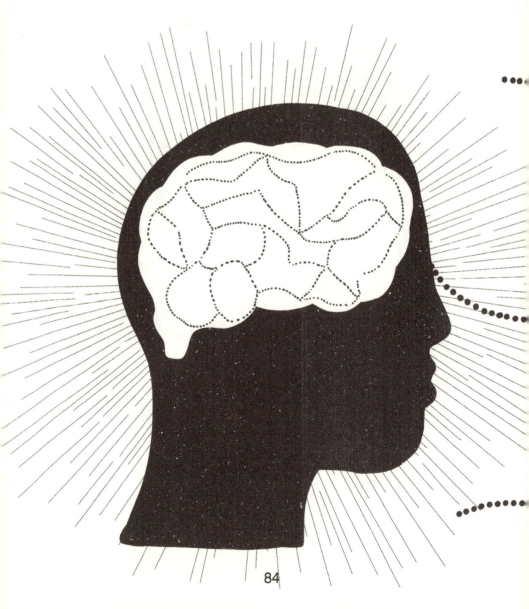

All your thoughts, feelings, habits, and behaviors reinforce the circuitry—known as neural pathways—in your brain. Your brain forms these neural pathways the same way hikers create trails through the forest. Paths rarely used became overgrown, hard to find, and eventually disappear. But the more hikers go on a certain path, the deeper, wider, and more established that path becomes. Similarly, everything you think, feel, or do trains the brain's neural pathways. Incredibly, new neural connections are formed throughout your entire life!

New activities and habits of thought create stronger neural pathways over time with repetition. Neurons that fire together wire together. By positioning your prayers toward positive ideals of gratitude, faith, and assurance, you enforce certain neural pathways in the brain, and create a habit of thought that ripples out into your life.

Habits of thought can motivate our actions in the world and create meaningful outcomes. 'Abdu'l-Bahá says, "The power of thought is dependent on its manifestation in deeds."[34]

Orienting our thoughts toward God's love and mercy helps us to see the world in a more hopeful light. It sensitizes the mind to perceive spiritual signs and confirmations, and helps us take constructive action.

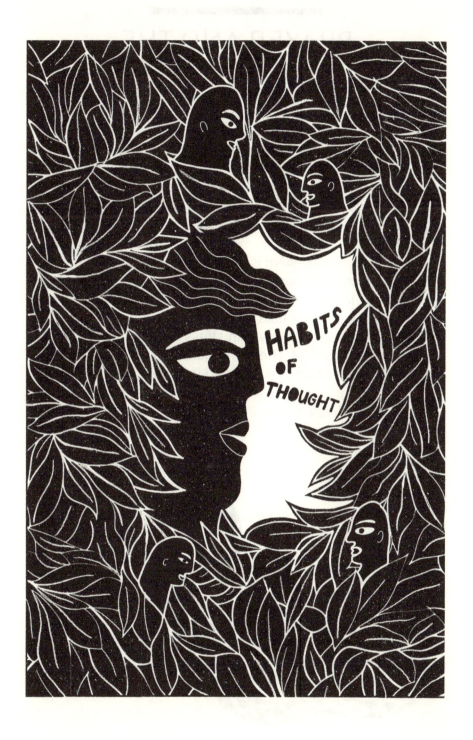

PRAYER AND THE NERVOUS SYSTEM

We are bombarded by sensory information every moment of the day. To survive, our brain must prioritize the input it receives; it must decide what needs to be focused on and what should be ignored. Prayer and reflection help your mind place your attention and energy wisely. This allows you to turn toward ideas and activities that align with your best self.

Your nervous system is designed to keep you safe. Your brain and nervous system are constantly scanning the environment for signs of threat or safety. If the nervous system perceives danger, it will take over the body's normal functioning and will flood your body with stress hormones such as adrenaline and cortisol. These hormones cause your breathing to quicken, your heart rate to speed up, your muscles to tense up, and your pupils to dilate. This is great if you need to react to an immediate threat!

However, various factors can cause us to get stuck in threat physiology (a.k.a. fight or flight) even when there's no immediate threat. This can cause chronic pain or anxiety. Recent brain research confirms that by giving our mind and body messages of safety, we can reinforce neural pathways that decrease the threat response and move us into safe physiology (a.k.a. rest and repair). This physically affects every cell of your body, as well as your state of mind.

The Bahá'í Faith places a strong emphasis on seeking the aid of skilled physicians or other professionals when dealing with physical or mental illness. We should seek the best help possible to get through psychological challenges. But there is also a spiritual dimension to healing.

"Sometimes, if the nervous system is paralyzed through fear, a spiritual remedy is necessary."

—'Abdu'l-Bahá[35]

Prayer and meditation are tools that can help create feelings of safety and support. They can help you connect to the bigger picture and strengthen your sacred connection with your Creator. A regulated nervous system can flow with the ups and downs of life. The physical nervous system is strengthened by spiritual faith, which can help you trust that the universe has your back and that everything will ultimately be okay. In a time of great upheaval, this sense of unwavering confidence is a gift to ourselves, our families, and our communities.

The development of our own individual soul takes place in connection with the time and place in which we live. Although we are surrounded by huge challenges and tragedies, the Bahá'í Faith offers a vision of radical hope.

CHAPTER FIVE

THE JOURNEY OF HUMANITY

One way of relating to the world is to assume that everything is arbitrary and pointless, and that history is just a random series of accidents that have led us to this point. However, the Bahá'í Faith teaches that history is a purposeful and evolving process guided by a divine plan, and that each stage in history is a step in humanity's spiritual development.

The evolution of consciousness over time is facilitated by a series of great teachers, called Manifestations of God, Who provide spiritual teachings that guide the individual and the greater society.

These teachers—such as Krishna, Zoroaster, Moses, Buddha, Christ, Muhammad, and Bahá'u'lláh—unleash the spiritual energy that advances humanity forward in every era. (Some of these Teachers we don't know the names of, as Their teachings were given orally or through symbols and rituals before the advent of written language.)

"All the Manifestations of God came with the same purpose, and they have all sought to lead men into the paths of virtue."

—'Abdu'l-Bahá[36]

The Manifestations emerge at different times and places in history, and progressively advance humanity's collective consciousness. These Figures are not regular people who are just way smarter than everyone else. As Manifestations of God, Their lives have a tremendous influence on the evolution of society. They release an outpouring of spirit that ripples across all of creation.

These great Teachers can be thought of as different lamps that shine with the same light. Their spiritual reality is one; but Their social teachings are different because they are based on the needs of the specific time and place where They lived. Each of these Beings reveals a different chapter in the story of one common religion, a concept referred to as

PROGRESSIVE REVELATION.[37]

This explains the Bahá'í belief in the oneness of religion.

The seasons of the natural world echo the regeneration of life brought by each Manifestation. Each of these great Teachers brings a divine springtime where new teachings regenerate the minds and hearts of society. Bahá'u'lláh's core teaching for our age is unity.

"The well-being of mankind, its peace and security are unattainable unless and until its unity is firmly established."

—Bahá'u'lláh[38]

The Bahá'í Faith says that God communicates with humanity not only through the sacred teachings of the Manifestations but also through nature. The beauty, order, and complexity of the natural world are expressions of God's attributes.

Nature serves as a reflection of divine qualities and provides insights into the Creator's wisdom and true beauty.

Bonding with nature can bring a sense of immediate connection with the awe-inspiring majesty of creation.

Nature demonstrates the wisdom of God in the material realm, while the Manifestations bring the wisdom of God from the spiritual realm. This is an expression of the inherent unity between the physical and spiritual dimensions of life.

The teachings of Manifestations serve as a holistic guide for personal spiritual development, as well as the enrichment of our wider society and culture. In this era, human civilization is going through an intense process of maturation.

THE WORLD IS IN TRANSITION

We live in an era in which technology is accelerating at a rapid pace, pushing beyond the limits of what anyone ever thought possible. For example, people used to ride around on bikes called Penny Farthings that looked absolutely ridiculous!

But now we have regular bikes!

And also the Large Hadron Collider.

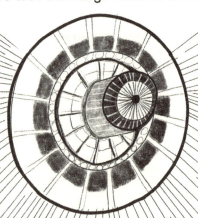

From a Bahá'í perspective, all of human history has led to this critical moment: Now is the time for humanity to strive toward greater and greater degrees of world peace, justice, and unity.

But if this is true, why are so many things falling apart? Why are people still divided by prejudice, racism, hatred, and violence?

NATURE shows us that AS ANY LIFE FORM GROWS and DEVELOPS, ITS PREVIOUS STATE CHANGES OR DECAYS.

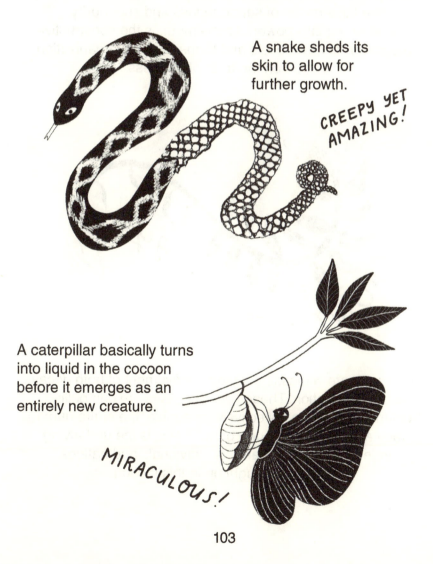

A snake sheds its skin to allow for further growth.

CREEPY YET AMAZING!

A caterpillar basically turns into liquid in the cocoon before it emerges as an entirely new creature.

MIRACULOUS!

What if the various crises we are currently experiencing right now as a global civilization represent the death of an old-world framework and the birth of a new one? What if the next phase of humanity's development is the collective recognition that we are all interdependent with the Earth and with each other?

According to the Bahá'í worldview, the evolution of consciousness is characterized by two powerful processes occurring simultaneously in the world right now. One is the *disintegration* of beliefs and social systems that are based on the false myths of separateness and superiority.
The other, equally powerful movement, is the constructive *integration* of new beliefs and forms of social organization based on the truth of oneness.

Today, we are witnessing a global movement of both decay and regeneration. These two processes are compelling humanity forward to collectively recognize "the entire human race as one soul and one body."[39] This is the underlying trajectory of history, and as individuals and nations, we are all caught up in this motion.

Civilization advances progressively, step-by-step. All religions speak of a promised time of peace, but this cool peace-world doesn't just drop from the sky out of nowhere. We build it ourselves, incrementally. This positive transformation is linked with an increase in emotional maturity and spiritual awareness.

The journey of humanity has taken place across isolated groups, tribes, nation-states, and empires, as we have built more complex forms of social organization. It's almost as if society has gone through different phases of collective infancy, childhood, and adolescence. Now, at this transition point into maturity, we are coming together to form a planetary civilization.[40]

The global forces of decay can feel overwhelming.
But they also function as a motivating force;
they can push us to work toward higher ideals.
This archetypal tension promotes growth—
it's a universal trope like a phoenix rising from the ashes,
or a lotus growing from the mud.

From a Bahá'í perspective, the elevation of our consciousness toward the unification of humanity is unstoppable. It's a trajectory that is embedded in the very blueprint of the universe.

Just like the blueprint of a tree is embedded in a seed!

Building greater degrees of world unity is a high ideal, and it depends upon the realization of the oneness of humanity.

THE ONENESS OF HUMANITY

We now have every scientific proof of the oneness of humanity. Human genome research shows that humans are genetically 99.9 percent the same. Our physical differences are seen in secondary traits such as eye color, hair texture, or melanin content. The idea of different human "races" is a misnomer. There is only one single human race, even though our ancestry is beautifully diverse.

FUN FACT:
ALL PEOPLE ON EARTH ARE RELATED AS DISTANT COUSINS!

Just as diverse ecosystems are stronger and more resilient than homogenous ones, human civilization is made stronger by protecting and preserving cultural diversity.

The belief that we are created by the same Source suggests there is a fundamental unity among all people. We are each given a divine soul by God and bound together in a sacred web of life.

While the oneness of humanity is a spiritual principle that's confirmed by science, different ideologies can stand in the way of recognizing this oneness. These mindsets create in-group and out-group categories, and people are seen as "good" or "bad" based on their culture, nationality, religion, or whatever.

When people feel anxious or uncertain about life, they can project their fears onto others. By scapegoating another group as the cause of their problems, people can justify violence, oppression, or just being obnoxious. People who are prejudiced are willfully committed to a form of ignorance, and as a result, they block their own spiritual development.

The fog of prejudice obscures the truth, and it causes us to see others as negative political abstractions rather than real human beings. 'Abdu'l-Bahá underscores that every war and conflict stems from the distortion of perception caused by prejudice.[41]

The Bahá'í writings describe a universal "crisis of identity" that can only be solved by recognizing our inherent oneness.

"Humanity is gripped by a crisis of identity, as various peoples and groups struggle to define themselves, their place in the world, and how they should act. Without a vision of shared identity and common purpose, they fall into competing ideologies and power struggles. Seemingly countless permutations of 'us' and 'them' define group identities ever more narrowly and in contrast to one another. Over time, this splintering into divergent interest groups has weakened the cohesion of society itself."

—The Universal House of Justice[42]

This global crisis of identity is resolved by recognizing that as a single humanity, we have a "shared identity and common purpose." But even if we know we are one interconnected human family, how can people rise above the anger or apathy they feel toward different groups? This level of social healing goes beyond a competition for power or technological fixes. It relates to the realm of the heart.

Building unity, through a Bahá'í lens, depends on a "mystic transformation."[43] The more one sees a reflection of the Divine in the souls of others, the easier it is to release prejudice and see others more clearly. Spiritual insight helps you to find points of unity with others, even amidst differences.[44]

A MYSTIC TRANSFORMATION OF THE HEART

Love is the force that holds the universe together, and ultimately, it's the most powerful thing that can bring us together. Aligning with the law of love opens doors that might otherwise be invisible.

We interact through relationships, so it makes sense that the work of social healing is inter-relational. The Bahá'í writings say that the principle of the oneness of humanity calls for "a complete reconceptualization of the relationships that sustain society."[45]

We long for relationships that are based in trust, solidarity, and love. Instead of adversarial approaches to social change, the Bahá'í focus is on finding what is unifying and constructive within relationships. Rather than using humiliation, coercion, or seeking power over others to achieve desired goals, we are called to build the unity we want to experience. Unity is not the final result in some faraway distant future, it's "the power through which these goals will be progressively realized."[46]

CHAPTER SIX

THE TWO-FOLD MORAL PURPOSE

a Bahá'í perspective, we each have a two-fold moral purpose: to attend to our own spiritual growth, and to contribute to the advancement of society through service to others. Through this two-fold purpose, spirituality and social action are joined together as one.

As individuals, we are impacted by the world around us. Our own beliefs and actions affect our communities, just as the structure of society influences us.

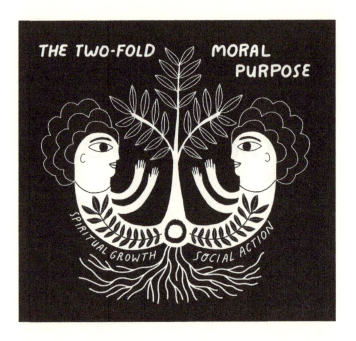

"We cannot segregate the human heart from the environment outside us and say that once one of these is reformed everything will be improved. Man is organic with the world. His inner life moulds the environment and is itself also deeply affected by it. The one acts upon the other and every abiding change in the life of man is the result of these mutual reactions."

—Shoghi Effendi[47]

One of the strangest aspects of quantum physics is entanglement, which Albert Einstein described as "spooky action at a distance."[48]

Entangled particles have a mysterious relationship: they influence each other instantaneously even if they are physically separated by a great distance.
No one understands how this is possible.

...ies are made of cells that are made of atoms that are ...e of subatomic particles. The particles that make up our entire physical reality exploded from stars and spread across the universe billions of years ago!

Are the particles within our bodies right now entangled in a state of intimate communion with the other particles on Earth and throughout the cosmos?

Is quantum entanglement an elegant metaphor, or something more? Even as the universe impacts us, do our thoughts and actions impact the universe in some way?

Is a shift of consciousness something that spreads between people? Can a thought or prayer travel the space between two souls?

Can the desire for love, unity, and justice be contagious?
When enough people embody these principles,
does society suddenly advance?

Likewise, can prejudice or cynicism also spread like a
contagion? And if so, how much more important is it to
focus on the positive reality you want to create?

"If you desire with all your heart,
friendship with every race on earth,
your thought, spiritual and positive,
will spread; it will become the desire of others,
growing stronger and stronger,
until it reaches the minds of all men."

—'Abdu'l-Bahá[49]

When things are a mess and there is no clear path out of the tangled knot of disfunction, it's difficult to know how to proceed. One way is to just burn it all down.

But the Bahá'í writings suggest that instead of trying to tear down what doesn't work, our whole energy should be directed "towards the building of the good, a good which has such a positive strength that in the face of it the multitude of evils—which are in essence negative—will fade away and be no more."[50]

As much as we may hate the bad things we see happening in the world, our motivation to transform society should be driven not by hatred but rather by our love of God, and we should arise to serve others "for the sake of God."[51]

Being of service for the sake of God means doing good without expecting a reward in heaven or fearing punishment in hell. It's not about trying to escape personal issues or striving to appear virtuous. Instead, serving with love is its own reward. There is a kind of fulfillment that comes when you align your spiritual principles with your actions in the world.

As individuals, we build the good through developing our spiritual virtues for the benefit of humanity. In this way, mystical love doesn't merely exist as a passive emotion; it finds expression in acts of connection and service.

Service to humanity is part of the very purpose of our creation. As Bahá'u'lláh has revealed,

"ALL MEN HAVE BEEN CREATED to CARRY FORWARD AN EVER-ADVANCING CIVILIZATION."
—BAHÁ'U'LLÁH [52]

The Bahá'í teachings also say: "Social change is not a project that one group of people carries out for the benefit of another."[53] Rather, it's a collaborative effort that encourages people to find common ground and walk side by side.

The Universal House of Justice has written, "Humanity's crying need will not be met by a struggle among competing ambitions or by protest against one or another of the countless wrongs afflicting a desperate age. It calls, rather, for a fundamental change of consciousness, for a wholehearted embrace of Bahá'u'lláh's teaching that the time has come when each human being on earth must learn to accept responsibility for the welfare of the entire human family."[54]

These are high ideals. But we need something to aim for in life, even if we can't always hit the target. We will always fall short of the highest ideal, but in a way, that's the point. When we strive for a high ideal, we work to bring our best self out to reach it.

Bahá'ís are aiming at two targets: we are seeking to discover the treasures of the inner world and striving to bring beauty and order to the outer world. The Bahá'í teachings do not recommend living in isolation and only focusing on your own inner spiritual life. Nor do they suggest that humanity's well-being will be achieved just through amazing material advancements. Both the material and the spiritual aspects of civilization need to progress in harmony.

Spiritual development is not about having magic, supernatural powers or being immune to difficulty or anxiety. It's about learning to harness these uncomfortable feelings and direct them toward constructive efforts. We're striving to bring love into the world through concrete actions.

Spiritual growth is not an escape from the harsh realities of the world; it is a pathway to a deeper understanding of these very realities.

It can bring renewed optimism to know that no matter how difficult things may get, the soul has limitless powers of resilience, creativity, and love, and we can express these powerful virtues in a way that's good.

"The honor and distinction of the individual consist in this, that he among all the world's multitudes should become a source of social good."

—'Abdu'l-Bahá[55]

The two-fold moral purpose connects the mystical yearnings of the soul with the urgent need for societal metamorphosis. It links our inner love of God with practical action in the world. As the old saying goes, we are called to "walk the mystical path with practical feet."[56]

CONCLUSION

As it turns out, no one has ever built a just and unified global civilization before. No one knows how to do it.

BUT WE DO NOT KNOW HOW TO BUILD WHATEVER IT IS WE ARE BUILDING!

The teachings of Bahá'u'lláh serve as a compass that can guide us along the path forward. As we navigate the path's twists and turns, we unearth the greater wisdom that's embedded in our victories and setbacks. We learn how to build upon what's already good and change what's not.

The Internet allows us an almost omniscient glimpse into everything happening in the world day by day. It's often overwhelming to take in all the alarming information that can drop into our awareness at any moment. Plus, so much information we receive is filtered through cynical, soul-crushing worldviews that feed outrage and hopelessness.

When the intensity of our times seems too much to handle,

Your heritage is in the stars and in the unknown realms of God's creation. An unfathomable series of events conspired over millennia to create the exact conditions from which your life emerged. Your life is part of the movement of the cosmos.

You have seen so much. You have felt sadness, rage, and fear, along with hope, grace, and joy. You know what it means to hurt others and to yourself be harmed. All these states of knowing are folded within you, and they can be a deep source of wisdom and insight.

As a soul living in this world, you are a seeker of truth—a spiritual being experiencing all the dramas of this stage of your development. Your soul is not a lone wanderer; you are part of a vast landscape of interconnected lives as humanity progresses through its difficult process of maturation. Your true self is a deep and eternal soul created by a merciful God.

Let the sick, broken, and destructive forces you experience in life be the soil into which you push your roots as you contribute to growing a better world. Those who are lost—the tyrants and the deceivers—can't take away the freedom of your soul.

Somehow the ever-abiding mystery of creation contains it all: everyone and everything, all the cruelty and the generosity. We are held in a paradox of growth: death and birth; decay and regeneration. Our shared stories become the raw material for sculpting new realities.

As a cosmic tree, your ever-expanding branches represent the infinite possibilities of existence, and your roots draw sustenance from the boundless energies of creation.

The Bahá'í teachings are not just for personal growth, they also provide a blueprint for building a new world. This transformation doesn't happen magically; it requires dedicated effort over time, despite many obstacles.

The Bahá'í Faith offers a story about what the world is going through that can bring relief and hope. This new narrative assures us that as one human family, we have a shared purpose and destiny.

May we continue to advance together, as expressed in this excerpt from a Bahá'í prayer for humanity:

O Thou kind Lord! Unite all. Let the religions agree and make the nations one, so that they may see each other as one family and the whole earth as one home. May they all live together in perfect harmony.

O God! Raise aloft the banner of the oneness of mankind.

O God! Establish the Most Great Peace.

Cement Thou, O God, the hearts together.

O Thou kind Father, God! Gladden our hearts through the fragrance of Thy love. Brighten our eyes through the Light of Thy Guidance. Delight our ears with the melody of Thy Word, and shelter us all in the Stronghold of Thy Providence.

Thou art the Mighty and Powerful, Thou art the Forgiving and Thou art the One Who overlooketh the shortcomings of all mankind.

—'Abdu'l-Bahá[57]

WHERE DO THESE BAHÁ'Í WRITINGS COME FROM?

The passages from the Bahá'í teachings cited in this book come from four main authors, the writings of each of whom form part of the authoritative cannon of Bahá'í writings. Below are brief descriptions of each:

Bahá'u'lláh (1817–1892), meaning in Arabic "the Glory of God," is the Prophet-Founder of the Bahá'í Faith, the youngest of the world's major independent religions. He was preceded by the Báb (1819–1850), His Forerunner Whose Writings also constitute part of Bahá'í scripture. Born in Persia (modern-day Iran), Bahá'u'lláh proclaimed His mission and station as a Messenger of God in 1863 and outlined a framework for developing a global civilization that takes into account both the spiritual and material dimensions of human life. His message, embraced by multitudes of people throughout His native Persia, was also met with severe opposition and persecution by the Muslim clergy and Persian government of the time and He lived a life of imprisonment and exile for forty years. Bahá'ís regard Him and the Báb as the most recent in a line of divine Prophets that includes Abraham, Krishna, Moses, Zoroaster, Buddha,

Christ, and Muhammad. The central theme of His message is that there is only one God, that all religions worship the same God, and that there is only one human race.

'Abdu'l-Bahá, meaning in Arabic "Servant of the Glory," is the title assumed by 'Abbas Effendi (1844–1921), the eldest son and appointed successor of Bahá'u'lláh. A prisoner since the age of nine, 'Abdu'l-Bahá shared a lifetime of imprisonment and exile with His Father at the hands of the Persian and Ottoman Empires. He spent His entire life in tireless service to, and promotion of, Bahá'u'lláh's teachings, and is considered by Bahá'ís to be the Perfect Exemplar of the Faith's teachings.

Shoghi Effendi (1897–1957) was the grandson and, along with the Universal House of Justice, one of the twin successors of 'Abdu'l-Bahá. He assumed his role as the Guardian of the Bahá'í Faith after the passing of 'Abdu'l-Bahá in 1921. Under his guidance, the Bahá'í community grew to global proportions and developed the framework of its administrative structure.

The Universal House of Justice is the international governing institution of the Bahá'í Faith. Originally conceived by Bahá'u'lláh, the Universal House of Justice was first elected in 1963. This administrative body is comprised of nine individuals who are elected every five years by members of national Bahá'í councils from across the globe.

THANK YOU

I would like to acknowledge a few of the many people who have been part of this creative process:

Donesh: Seriously, I couldn't have done this without you! Thanks for sharing your wise and expansive mind and heart.

Mahku and Tammy: It's an honor to know you both and share so many wild adventures together!

Everyone in our youth group: It's amazing to watch you all grow and come together in such a positive way!

Narmin and Derik: Thanks for the millions of conversations and helping me sort my brain out over the years.

Bahhaj, Chris, and Nat: Thanks for going through the intense editing process with me and helping me to bring this book to life!

The Springdale Bahá'í community: Thank you for being so vibrant and epic.

Kazimir and Zarek: Pieces of my heart walking around outside my body.

Nick: Thank you for your support and love.

Finally: Mae, Nima, Mackenzie, Emma, Shamil, Varqa, Walter, Nate, Lenette, Carla, Naomi, Amalia, Farida, Niaz, and our dear Lucho. It's an honor to collaborate with all of you!

AFTERWORD

For a long time, I've wanted to write and illustrate a book about the Bahá'í Faith and I'm happy I had this opportunity. I have been a Bahá'í for about twenty-five years, having learned about the Faith initially in my early teens. I was raised very secular, with an interest in changing the world and an openness to spirituality. As a young person I had a somewhat intense disposition, and once I started studying the Bahá'í Faith, I decided that I needed to know everything possible about it to determine if I could accept it. I changed my course of study in college so that I could focus on religion. I read many books and I grappled with the overall implications of Bahá'u'lláh's teachings.

I found that everything I was learning about the Bahá'í Faith was somehow in direct conversation with events that were unfolding in my life. In the realm of social activism, I wondered how we could make positive change when not only were our perceived enemies so strong, but there was so much infighting and division amongst ourselves as activists. I longed for some kind of transcendent vision that could pull me out of the spiral of constant fear, criticism, and suspicion of others (and myself) that characterized my so-called "radical" approach to the world.

At the same time, I had always felt a connection with something greater than myself, and I was very dedicated to exploring the spiritual dimension of existence. I spent many years involved with Buddhist practice as well as Sufi mysticism and various other spiritual modalities. What troubled me is that I wasn't sure how my spiritual explorations related to my activist aspirations, and just everyday living.

For my entire life I had heard about the evils of "organized religion," and I had a massive prejudice against it. I saw it as a mental crutch for people who were too weak to think for themselves, or as an oppressive force meant to control and dominate people. A friend of mine had recently joined the Bahá'í Faith and we started having very deep conversations about the purpose of life, the existence of God, and the meaning of religion. It wasn't long after this that I started to study religion in school. I mostly focused on the Abrahamic religions: Judaism, Christianity, and Islam. It was at this point I had to recognize how little I really knew about religious history or any of these traditions.

As I continued to learn, I found that the Bahá'í perspective cast all my previous ideas about religion into a new light. I no longer thought of the major religions as a bunch of competing groups, but rather saw them each as part of a single unfolding process. The Bahá'í teachings were an antidote to the hopeless doom-and-gloom attitudes of some of the ideologies I was wrapped up in, and helped me see that true spirituality combines inner growth with hopeful action in the world. Although I couldn't easily perceive it, I was undergoing a mysterious, mystical transformation at this time. I felt deeply moved by Bahá'u'lláh's writings and soon felt that I wanted to commit myself to the Bahá'í laws and teachings. Basically, I fell in love.

Twenty-five years later, my relationship with the Bahá'í Faith has changed and deepened. The global Bahá'í community turns to the Universal House of Justice for guidance that is delivered to us in a series of plans. In our current Nine Year Plan, the fundamental goal is to release the society-building powers of the Faith in greater and greater measures. In this pursuit, Bahá'ís worldwide collaborate with people of all walks of life in the process of community building. Together, we are all learning how to apply spiritual principles to our own lives, as well as read reality and consult on how to address different issues in our neighborhoods and communities.

The times we are living in are marked by a crisis of meaning as things change so fast and our old models of understanding no longer make sense. People long for a sense of belonging and a community that they can trust. While our first impulse may be to look for some ready-built utopian group where we can finally relax, the truth is that these times call for us each to be protagonists to help build more meaningful and unified spaces that embrace a growing number of people.

Because we are human, these efforts will always be filled with layers of complexity and challenge. There will be ongoing cycles of crisis and victory. But, as we continue to build a shared vision, things get a little easier. Bahá'u'lláh has offered a renewed conceptual framework for this era, and teachings designed to summon our best selves. Whatever your background, may this book bring you a sense of hope!

Misha Blaise
May 2024

NOTES

IMPORTANT NOTE

1. 'Abdu'l-Bahá, in *Bahá'í Prayers,* p. 216.

INTRODUCTION

2. 'Abdu'l-Bahá, *The Promulgation of Universal Peace,* p. 372.

CHAPTER 1: THE LIFE OF THE SOUL

3. Eckhart Tolle expresses a similar idea in *The Power of Now: A Guide to Spiritual Enlightenment.* Tolle's words are: "You are the Universe expressing itself as a human for a little while."

4. 'Abdu'l-Bahá, *Selections from the Writings of 'Abdu'l-Bahá,* no. 21.6.

5. Ibid., *Paris Talks,* no. 29.3.

6. Ibid., in *Lights of Guidance,* no. 691.

7. See Bahá'u'lláh, *Gleanings from the Writings of Bahá'u'lláh,* no. 80.

CHAPTER 2: THE SOUL'S RELATIONSHIP WITH GOD

8. God transcends any biological category of male or female. English translations of the Bahá'í writings use male pronouns to refer to God in accordance with literary conventions. Bahá'í guidance states that "the Writings of Bahá'u'lláh . . . portray both the transcendence and immanence of God," and that "the entire question of sex in this context falls into total insignificance." From a letter written on behalf of the Universal House of Justice to an individual, dated 24 October 1996.

9. Bahá'u'lláh, *Gleanings from the Writings of Bahá'u'lláh,* no. 153.5.

10. From a letter written on behalf of Shoghi Effendi, dated 8 December 1935, to an individual, in *Lights of Guidance,* no. 1704.

11. Bahá'u'lláh, *Gleanings from the Writings of Bahá'u'lláh,* no. 125.1.

12. Joseph Adu-Amankwaah, "'Happy Heart' Versus 'Broken Heart' Syndrome: The 2 Faces of Takotsubo Syndrome: Similarities and Differences," *Journal of the American College of Cardiology: Heart Failure, Volume 10, Issue 7,* 2022, pp. 467–69.

13. 'Abdu'l-Bahá, *Selections from the Writings of 'Abdu'l-Bahá,* no. 12.1.

14. See 'Abdu'l-Bahá, *The Promulgation of Universal Peace,* pp. 195–96.

CHAPTER 3: TESTS AND DIFFICULTIES

15. Bahá'u'lláh, in *Bahá'í Prayers,* "Fire Tablet," p. 317.

16. From a letter written on behalf of Shoghi Effendi, dated 30 June 1923, to an individual believer, in *Lights of Guidance,* no. 2048.

17. Leo Babauta, "The Obstacle is the Path," https://zenhabits.net/obstacle/, accessed 2/23/2024.

18. Bahá'u'lláh, The Hidden Words, Arabic no. 13.

19. 'Abdu'l-Bahá, Paris Talks, no. 18.2.

20. Bahá'u'lláh, Tablets of Bahá'u'lláh, p. 118.

21. Shoghi Effendi, Directives from the Guardian, no. 207.

22. Bahá'u'lláh, Tablets of Bahá'u'lláh, p. 34.

23. Bessel van der Kolk, The Body Keeps the Score: Brain, Mind, and Body in the Healing of Trauma, p. 38.

CHAPTER 4: HOW TO TRANSFORM

24. From a letter written on behalf of Shoghi Effendi, dated 11 April 1947, to the National Spiritual Assembly of the United States: Insert with Bahá'í News, no. 232, June 1950, in Lights of Guidance, no. 2061.

25. Bahá'u'lláh, Tablets of Bahá'u'lláh, p. 173.

26. Ibid., Gleanings from the Writings of Bahá'u'lláh, no. 125.6.

27. Walt Whitman, Song of Myself, 51, at https://poets.org/poem/song-myself-51, accessed 2/23/2024.

28. Bahá'u'lláh, The Hidden Words, Arabic no.4.

29. 'Abdu'l-Bahá, in Bahá'í Prayers, p. 70.

30. Bahá'u'lláh, The Kitáb-i-Íqán, ¶164.

31. 'Abdu'l-Bahá, in the Diary of Mirzá Ahmad Sohrab, 15 March 1914, in Star of the West, vol. 9, no. 4, pp. 103–4.

32. 'Abdu'l-Bahá, Paris Talks, no. 26.7.

33. Ibid., no. 54.13.

34. Ibid., no. 2.6.

35. Ibid., 'Abdu'l-Bahá in London, p. 60.

CHAPTER 5: THE JOURNEY OF HUMANITY

36. 'Abdu'l-Bahá, *Paris Talks,* no. 39.6.

37. Bahá'u'lláh, *Gleanings from the Writings of Bahá'u'lláh,* no. 31.1.

38. Ibid., no. 131.2.

39. Ibid., no. 107.1.

40. See the Universal House of Justice, letter dated 2 March 2013, to the Bahá'ís of Iran.

41. 'Abdu'l-Bahá, *Selections from the Writings of 'Abdu'l-Bahá,* no. 227.11.

42. The Universal House of Justice, from a letter dated 18 January 2019, to the Bahá'ís of the world.

43. Bahá'u'lláh, The Kitáb-i-Íqán, ¶164.

44. The Bahá'í community in Iran exemplifies how to take a non-adversarial approach to social change amidst violent persecution. Their approach is described in an essay by Michael Karlberg. See Michael Karlberg, "Constructive Resilience: The Bahá'í Response to Oppression," *Peace & Change, Vol. 35, No. 2,* April 2010.

45. The Universal House of Justice, from a letter dated 2 March 2013, to the Bahá'ís of Iran.

46. *One Common Faith,* p. 54.

CHAPTER 6: THE TWO-FOLD MORAL PURPOSE

47. From a letter written on behalf of Shoghi Effendi, dated 17 February 1933, to an individual believer, at https://www.bahai.org/beliefs/essential-relationships/individual-society/quotations, accessed 2/23/2024.

48. See Andreas Muller, "What is quantum entanglement? A physicist explains Einstein's 'spooky action at a distance,'" at https://www.astronomy.com/science/what-is-quantum-entanglement-a-physicist-explains-einsteins-spooky-action-at-a-distance/.

49. 'Abdu'l-Bahá, *Paris Talks,* no. 6.11.

50. From a letter written on behalf of the Universal House of Justice, dated 19 November 1974, to the National Spiritual Assembly of Italy, in *Lights of Guidance,* no. 415.

51. The Universal House of Justice, letter dated 25 March 1975, to all National Spiritual Assemblies, in *Lights of Guidance,* no. 2138.

52. Bahá'u'lláh, *Gleanings from the Writings of Bahá'u'lláh,* no. 109.2.

53. The Universal House of Justice, message to the Bahá'ís of the world, Ridván 2010.

54. The Universal House of Justice, letter dated 24 May 2001, to the Believers Gathered for the Events Marking the Completion of the Projects on Mount Carmel, in *Turning Point: Selected Messages of the Universal House of Justice and Supplementary Material, 1996–2006,* no. 26.6.

55. 'Abdu'l-Bahá, *The Secret of Divine Civilization,* p. 5.

56. This phrase is similar to the words of a reporter for the Palo Altan newspaper reporting on 'Abdu'l-Bahá's visit to Standford, which reads, "Abbas Effendi leads his followers over what is elsewhere called the Mystic Way; but wherever they march, they tread with practical feet." See https://centenary.bahai.us/news/abdul-baha-bahai-prophet-speaks-stanford-university.

CONCLUSION

57. 'Abdu'l-Bahá, in *Bahá'í Prayers,* pp. 113–15.

BIBLIOGRAPHY

WORKS OF BAHÁ'U'LLÁH

Gleanings from the Writings of Bahá'u'lláh. Translated by Shoghi Effendi. Wilmette, IL: Bahá'í Publishing, 2005.

The Hidden Words. Translated by Shoghi Effendi. Wilmette, IL: Bahá'í Publishing, 2002.

The Kitáb-i-Íqán: The Book of Certitude. Translated by Shoghi Effendi. Wilmette, IL: Bahá'í Publishing, 2003.

Tablets of Bahá'u'lláh revealed after the Kitáb-i-Aqdas. Compiled by the Research Department of the Universal House of Justice. Translated by Habib Taherzadeh et al. Wilmette, IL: Bahá'í Publishing Trust, 1988.

WORKS OF 'ABDU'L-BAHÁ

'Abdu'l-Bahá in London: Addresses and Notes of Conversations. London: Bahá'í Publishing Trust, 1982.

Paris Talks: Addresses Given By 'Abdu'l-Bahá in Paris in 1911. Wilmette, IL: Bahá'í Publishing, 2011.

Promulgation of Universal Peace: Talks Delivered by 'Abdu'l-Bahá during His Visit to the United States and Canada in 1912. Compiled by Howard MacNutt. Wilmette, IL: Bahá'í Publishing, 2012.

The Secret of Divine Civilization. Translated by Marzieh Gail and Ali-Kuli Khan. Wilmette, IL: Bahá'í Publishing, 2007.

Selections from the Writings of 'Abdu'l-Bahá. Compiled by the Research Department of the Universal House of Justice. Translated by a Committee at the Bahá'í World Center and Marzieh Gail. Wilmette, IL: Bahá'í Publishing, 2010.

WORKS OF SHOGHI EFFENDI

Directives from the Guardian. Wilmette, IL: Bahá'í Publishing Trust, 1973.

WORKS OF THE UNIVERSAL HOUSE OF JUSTICE

Messages from the Universal House of Justice, 2001–2022: The Fifth Epoch of the Formative Age. Evanston, IL: Bahá'í Publishing, 2024.

Turning Point: 1996–2006, Selected Messages of the Universal House of Justice and Supplementary Material. West Palm Beach, FL: Palabra, 2006.

BAHÁ'Í COMPILATIONS

Bahá'í Prayers: A Selection of Prayers Revealed by Bahá'u'lláh, the Báb, and 'Abdu'l-Bahá. New ed. Wilmette, IL: Bahá'í Publishing Trust, 2002.

Lights of Guidance: A Bahá'í Reference File. Compiled by Helen Hornby. New ed. New Delhi, India: Bahá'í Publishing Trust, 1994.

OTHER WORKS

Adu-Amankwaah, Joseph. "'Happy Heart' Versus 'Broken Heart' Syndrome: The 2 Faces of Takotsubo Syndrome: Similarities and Differences," *Journal of the American College of Cardiology: Heart Failure, Volume 10, Issue 7,* 2022.

Karlberg, Michael. "Constructive Resilience: The Bahá'í Response to Oppression," *Peace & Change, Vol. 35, No. 2,* April 2010.

One Common Faith. Prepared under the supervision of the Universal House of Justice. Wilmette, IL: Bahá'í Publishing Trust, 2005.

Star of the West, The Bahá'í Magazine, Periodical. 25 vols. 1910–1935. Vols. 1–14. Oxford: George Ronald, 1978. Online: http://bahai.works/Star_of_the_West.

Tolle, Eckhart. *The Power of Now: A Guide to Spiritual Enlightenment.* Novata, California: New World Library, 2004.

van der Kolk, Bessel. *The Body Keeps the Score: Brain, Mind, and Body in the Healing of Trauma.* Penguin, 2014.